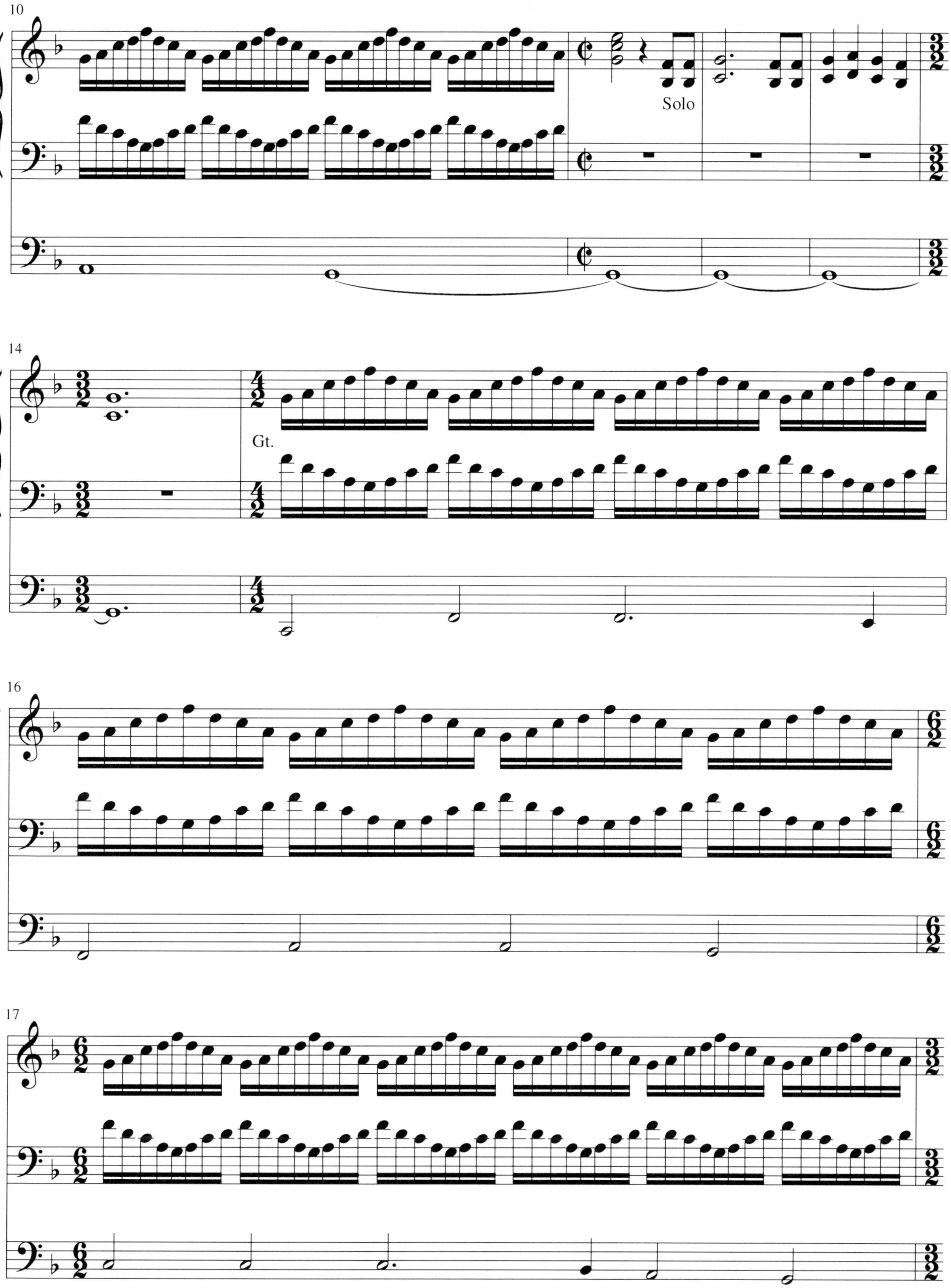
10
Solo
14
Gt.
16
17

18
Positiv
Reduce Ped. -32', large reeds
stringendo
from "Prelude in G Major," BWV 625 - J. S. Bach
23
♩ = 84
Great
-Sw. Reeds
26
28

30
33
36
39

42
45
48
Pos.
52
Swell: Full (Box closed)
Gt.
Great
Open Swell
Pedal: Add